THIS WALKER BOOK

JENKINS, M.

Chameleons are cool

514          Pbk

Please return/renew this item by the last date shown

worcestershire
c o u n t y c o u n c i l
Cultural Services

D0414529

Chameleons are lizards,
and lizards are reptiles,
like snakes, crocodiles and tortoises.
There are about 4,000 kinds
of lizard altogether, including
around 120 different chameleons.
Just over half of all the kinds
of chameleon come from Madagascar,
a big island off the east coast of Africa.
Most of the others live in
mainland Africa.

First published 1997 by
Walker Books Ltd
87 Vauxhall Walk
London SE11 5HJ

This edition published 1999

2 4 6 8 10 9 7 5 3 1

Text © 1997 Martin Jenkins
Illustrations © 1997 Sue Shields

This book has been typeset in Calligraphic and Soupbone.

Printed in Singapore

British Library Cataloguing in Publication Data
A catalogue record for this book is
available from the British Library.

ISBN 0-7445-6333-X

# CHAMELEONS ARE COOL

Martin Jenkins

illustrated by
Sue Shields

WALKER BOOKS
AND SUBSIDIARIES
LONDON • BOSTON • SYDNEY

Geckos' toes are as sticky as Velcro.

Some lizards eat bananas — chameleons don't. Some lizards walk upside down on the ceiling — chameleons can't. There's even a lizard that glides from tree to tree — a chameleon certainly wouldn't do that!

The flying lizard glides on wing-like flaps of skin.

Iguanas don't just eat bananas. They love all sorts of fruit.

6

But of all the different kinds of lizard,
I still think chameleons are the best.

Chameleons are cool.

It's not that they're all that big.
The biggest is only about
the size of a rather small cat.
It's called Oustalet's chameleon
and it lives in Madagascar.

Whatever their size, chameleons usually
get sick and die if kept as pets.
They're much better off left in the wild.

8

They can be really really small, though.
The smallest one could
balance happily on your
little finger. It's called
the Dwarf Brookesia,
and it lives in
Madagascar, too.

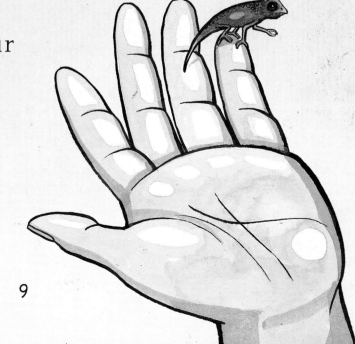

And I suppose you wouldn't exactly call many of them beautiful. Their skin is wrinkly and bumpy, and they've got big bulgy eyes, while lots of them have the most ridiculous...

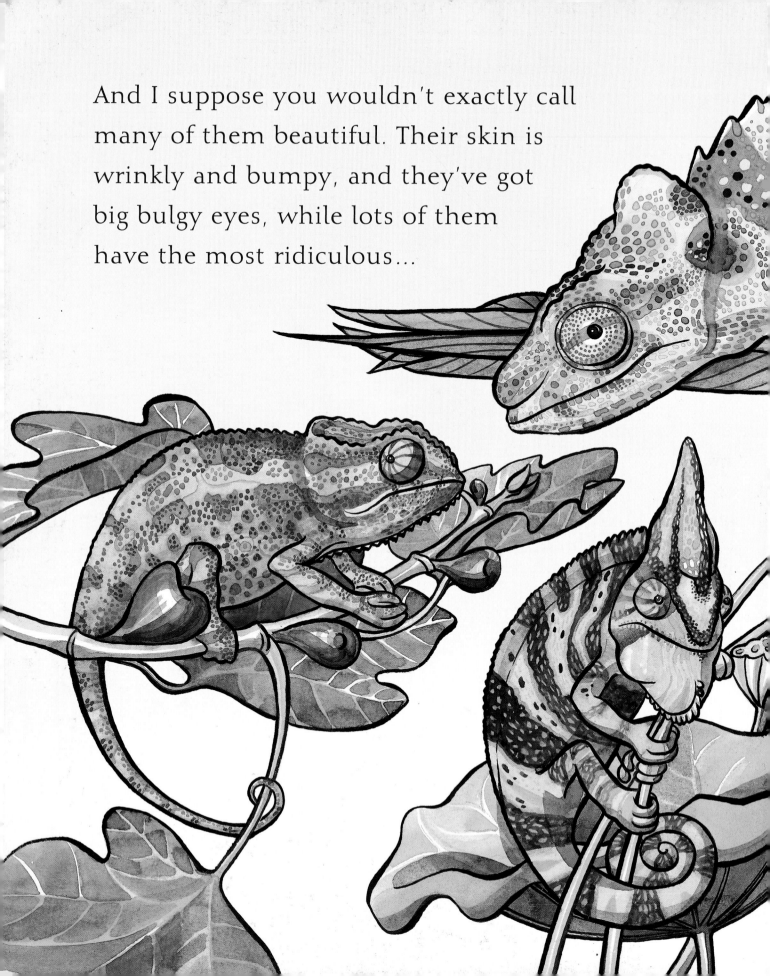

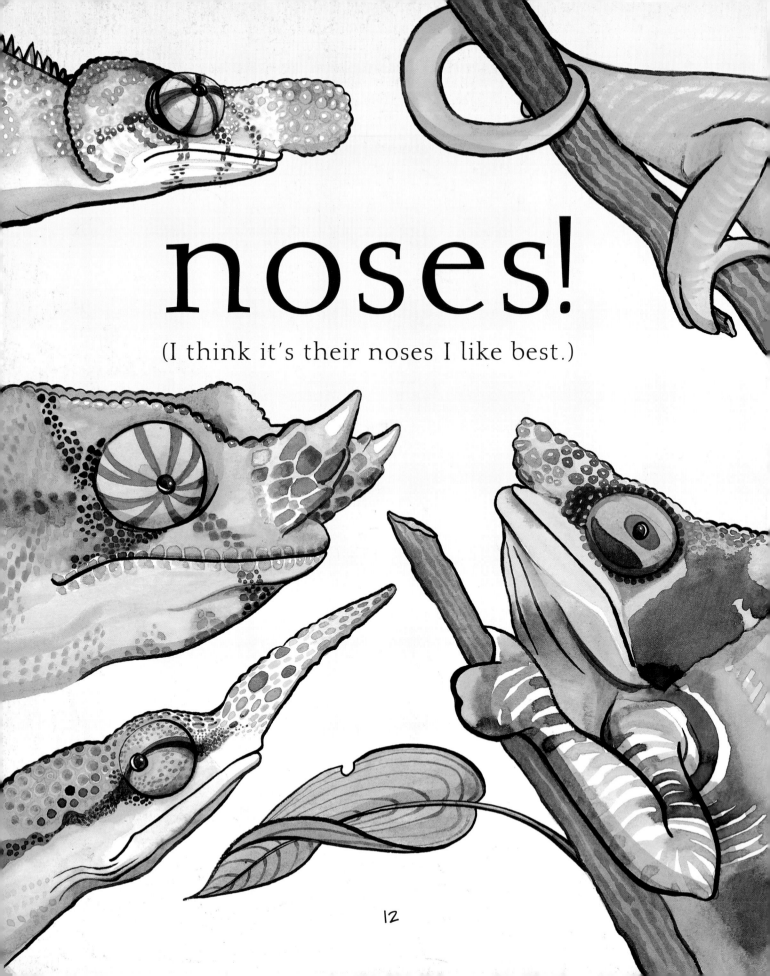

# noses!

(I think it's their noses I like best.)

Their mouths are pretty odd, too.
They turn down at the corners,
which is why chameleons
always look grumpy.

Actually they don't just look grumpy.
They **are** grumpy.
So if two chameleons bump into each other,
things can get pretty lively. There's lots
of puffing and hissing — and sometimes,
there's a real fight.

A chameleon will only fight with the same kind of chameleon as itself.

And that's when chameleons do what they're most famous for — they change colour.

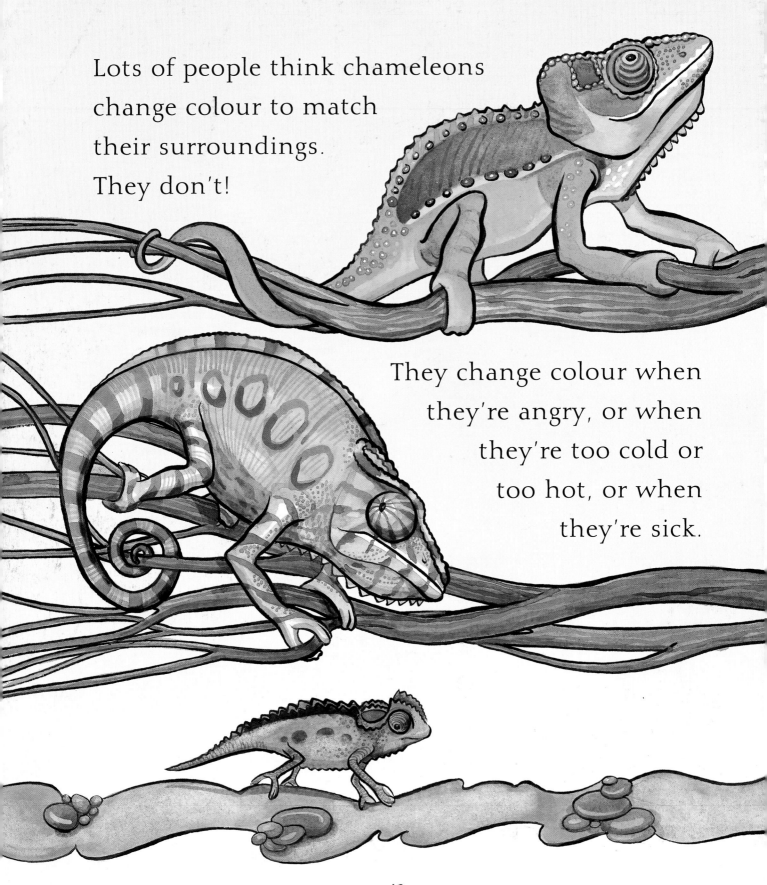

Lots of people think chameleons change colour to match their surroundings. They don't!

They change colour when they're angry, or when they're too cold or too hot, or when they're sick.

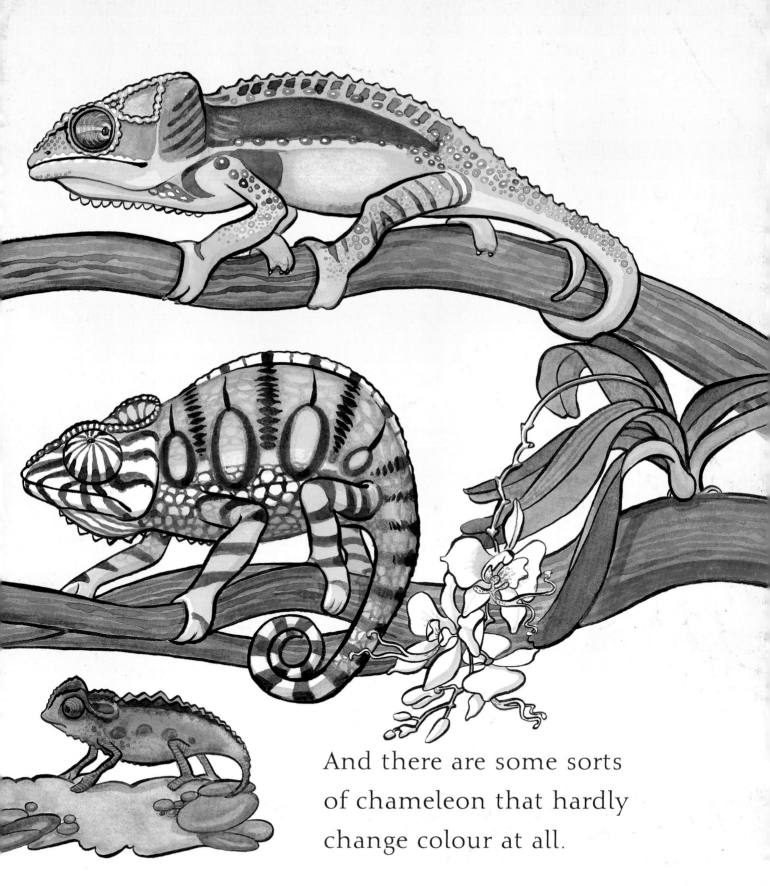

And there are some sorts
of chameleon that hardly
change colour at all.

As a rule, though, chameleons don't bump
into each other all that often. I suppose
it wouldn't be fair to call them lazy,
but they certainly don't move
any more than they have to.
And when they do,
it's almost always
incredibly
slowly.

A chameleon's feet are shaped
like pincers for holding on
tightly to branches.

Sometimes they stop completely,
in mid-step, as if they've
quite forgotten what they're
supposed to be doing.

But if you look closely
you'll see that they're actually
carefully peering about.

Now, peering about is something chameleons
are rather good at. That's because
their eyes can move separately
from each other, unlike
our eyes which always
move together.

Most of a chameleon's eye is covered in skin, like the rest of its body.

There's a tiny peep-hole in the middle that the chameleon sees through.

22

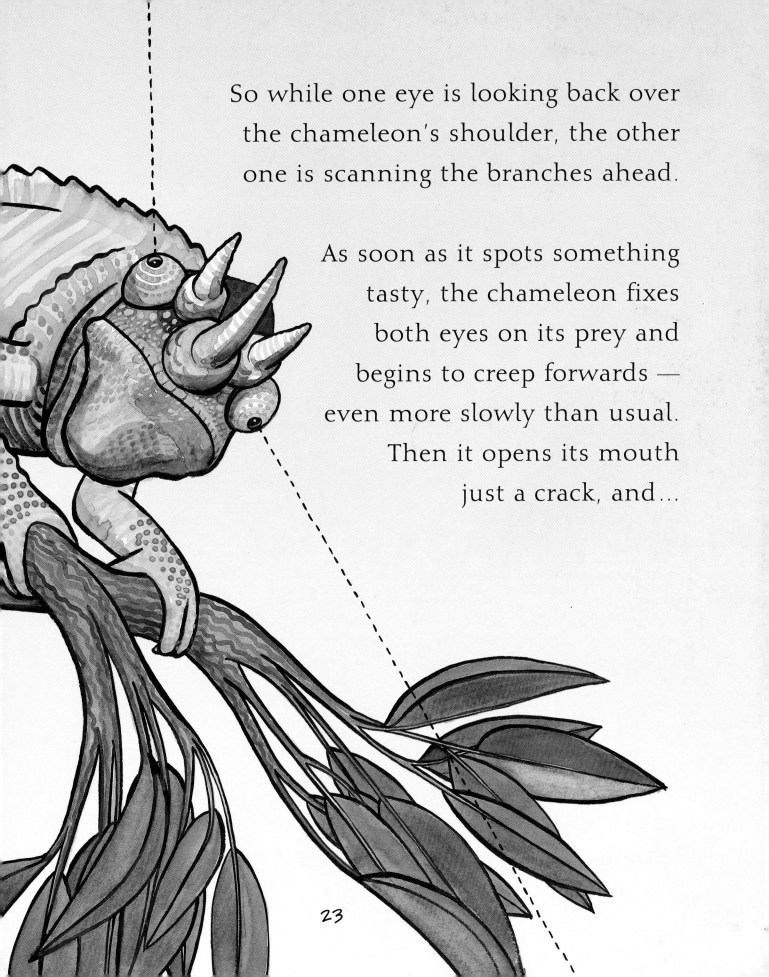

So while one eye is looking back over the chameleon's shoulder, the other one is scanning the branches ahead.

As soon as it spots something tasty, the chameleon fixes both eyes on its prey and begins to creep forwards — even more slowly than usual. Then it opens its mouth just a crack, and...

23

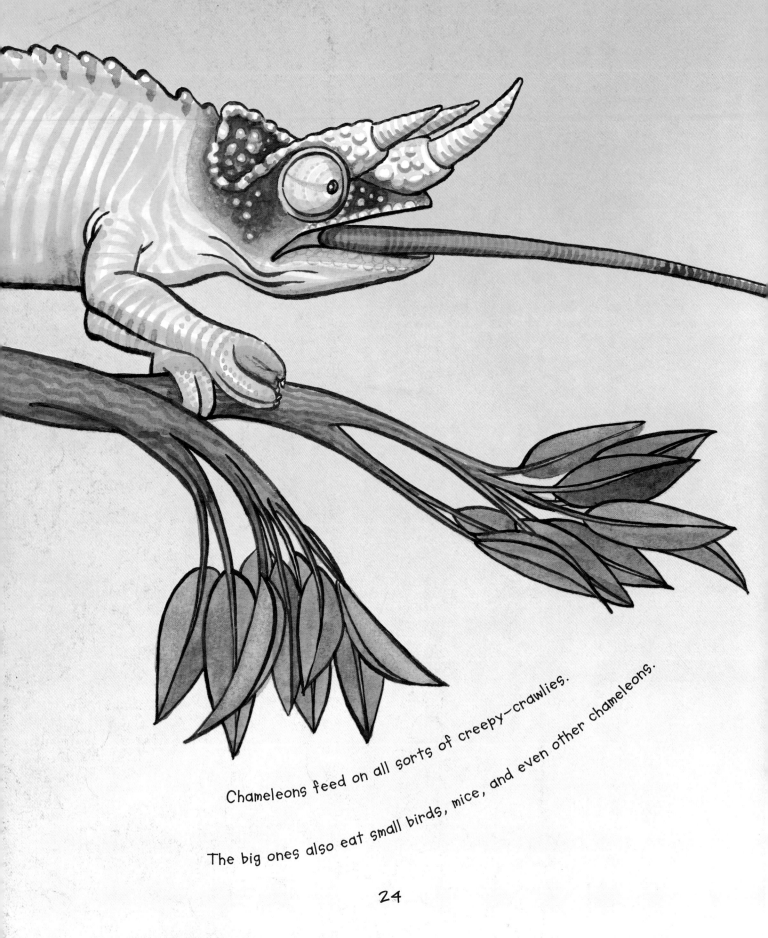

Chameleons feed on all sorts of creepy-crawlies.

The big ones also eat small birds, mice, and even other chameleons.

24

Out shoots this amazingly long tongue,
with a sticky bit at the end, like a piece
of well-chewed chewing gum.

# thwap!

Then the tongue flies back,
and there's a lot
of chomping
and chewing,
and perhaps
a few bits
of insect leg
fluttering to the ground.

Most lizards gulp their food down without chewing it, but chameleons grind everything up thoroughly!

And after that the chameleon
just sits there for an hour or two,
doing nothing very much at all,
looking quite exhausted (and still
grumpy) after all that hard work.

And there you have it.
How could you possibly
resist a pocket-sized,
bad-tempered, colour-changing,
swivel-eyed, snail-paced,
long-tongued sharp-shooter?

If chameleons aren't cool,
then I don't know what is!

# Index

Look up the pages to find out about
all these chameleon things.
Don't forget to look at both kinds
of word — this kind and this kind.

# About the Author

Martin Jenkins is a conservation biologist, who works for
agencies such as the World Wide Fund For Nature.
"When I first saw chameleons in the wild in Madagascar,"
he recalls, "I fell in love with them at first sight.
I picked one up, ever so gently, and it promptly bit me
on the thumb. I still think they're wonderful, but tend
to leave them alone whenever I bump into them!"
Martin is also the author of *Fly Traps! Plants that bite back* and
*Wings, Stings and Wriggly Things*, a BRIGHT SPARKS book
about minibeasts.

# About the Illustrator

Award-winning illustrator Sue Shields has worked
on everything from posters to murals, shop interiors,
magazines, newspapers, greetings cards and children's books.
For *Chameleons are Cool*, she had to adapt her use
of watercolour, "to try to describe not only
their astonishing colours, but a hint of the colours they
can change to". And although she won't give
any names, she says that the chameleons' faces kept
reminding her of people she knows!

# MORE WALKER PAPERBACKS
## For You to Enjoy

### WALK WITH A WOLF
by Janni Howker/Sarah Fox-Davies

Shortlisted for the Kurt Maschler Award

Come with award-winning author Janni Howker on a spellbinding journey to the far,
wild north and meet one of the world's most magnificent, yet misunderstood, creatures.

"Any book by this author deserves attention… There is no sentiment in this impressive book,
but you will share her sense of respect." *The Times Educational Supplement*

0-7445-6334-8    £4.99

### BIG BLUE WHALE
by Nicola Davies/Nick Maland

Voyage into the world of the blue whale to discover what it
sounds like, feels like, even what it smells like.

"This is a marvellous meeting with a blue whale; it fills the reader with a sense
of wonder and the drawings are at once lucid and eccentric.
It's stranger than any fiction." *The Observer*

0-7445-6300-3    £4.99

### FLY TRAPS! PLANTS THAT BITE BACK
by Martin Jenkins/David Parkins

Shortlisted for the Times Educational Supplement's Junior Information Book Award

This is a captivating introduction to the world of carnivorous plants – squishy bladderworts and
sticky sundews, cobra lillies, pitcher plants, snapping Venus flytraps and lots more.

0-7445-5286-9    £4.99